Bilingual Picture Dictionaries

My First Book of
Portuguese Words

by Katy R. Kudela

Translator: Translations.com

apple
maçã
(mah-SAN)

CAPSTONE PRESS
a capstone imprint

Table of Contents

How to Use This Dictionary

This book is full of useful words in both Portuguese and English. The English word appears first, followed by the Portuguese word. Look below each Portuguese word for help to sound it out. Try reading the words aloud.

Topic Heading in English

Topic Heading in Portuguese

Word in English
Word in Portuguese
(pronunciation)

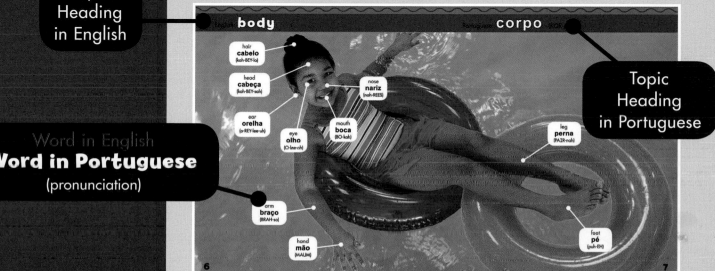

English: **body**   Portuguese: **corpo** (KOR

hair
cabelo
(kah-BEY-lo)

head
cabeça
(kah-BEY-sah)

nose
nariz
(nah-REES)

ear
orelha
(o-REY-lee-uh)

eye
olho
(O-lee-oh)

mouth
boca
(BO-kah)

leg
perna
(PAIR-nah)

arm
braço
(BRAH-so)

hand
mão
(MAUM)

foot
pé
(puh-EH)

6   7

Notes about the Portuguese Language

The Brazilian Portuguese language uses the same alphabet as English. Most letters are read the same. There are some letter combinations that sound different. These include:

ch (sh)   lh (li)   nh (ny)

The Portuguese language uses accents, shown with a ^, ~, or ´. The accents mean that your voice should stress the vowel with the accent.

uncle
tio
(TEE-oh)

mother
mãe
(MA-ee)

cousin
primo
(PREE-mo)

aunt
tia
(TEE-ah)

baby
bebê
(bey-BEY)

4

Portuguese: família (fah-MEE-lee-uh)

grandmother
avó
(ah-VOH)

father
pai
(PA-ee)

grandfather
avô
(ah-VOU)

brother
irmão
(ir-MAUM)

sister
irmã
(ir-MAN)

5

hair
cabelo
(kah-BEY-lo)

head
cabeça
(kah-BEY-sah)

ear
orelha
(o-REY-lee-uh)

eye
olho
(O-lee-oh)

nose
nariz
(nah-REES)

mouth
boca
(BO-kah)

arm
braço
(BRAH-so)

hand
mão
(MAUM)

leg
perna
(PAIR-nah)

foot
pé
(puh-EH)

pajamas
pijama
(pee-JAM-ah)

coat
casaco
(kah-ZA-ko)

shorts
bermuda
(ber-MOO-dah)

boot
bota
(BOW-tah)

ROAR!
I'm the Loudest in the Jungle

shoe
sapato
(sah-PA-to)

hat
chapéu
(chah-PAI-oo)

pants
calça
(CAU-sah)

sock
meia
(MEY-ah)

dress
vestido
(ves-TEE-do)

shirt
camiseta
(ka-mee-ZEY-tah)

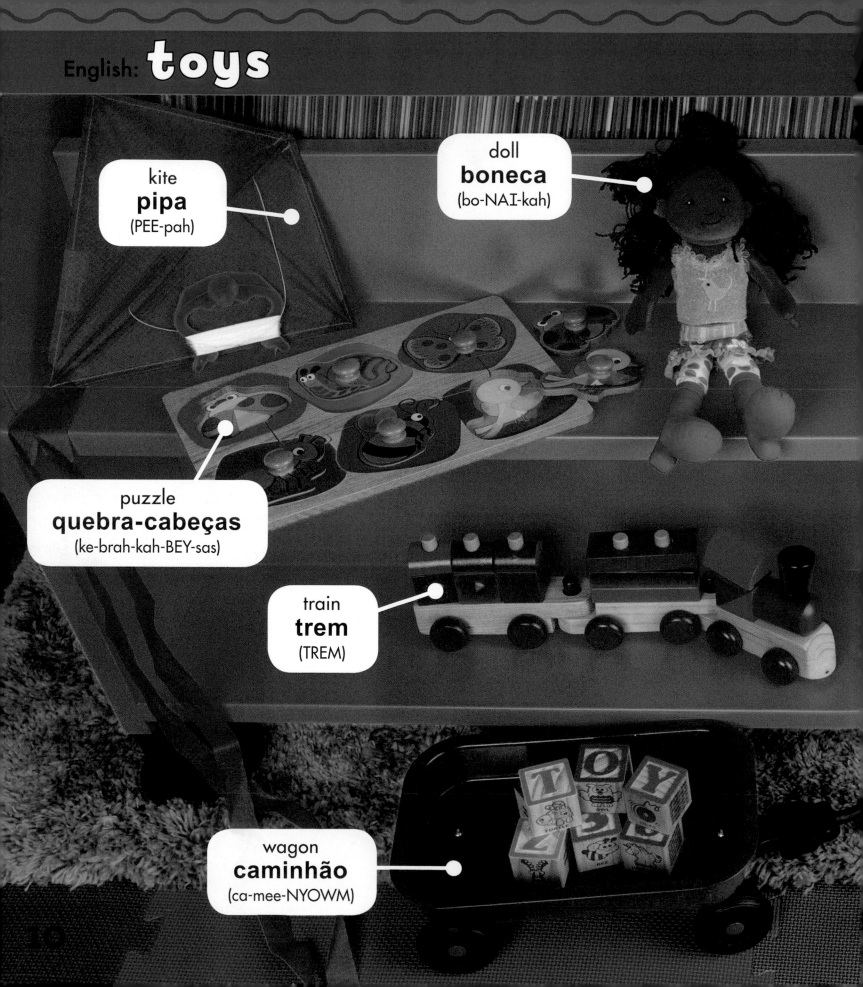

kite
pipa
(PEE-pah)

doll
boneca
(bo-NAI-kah)

puzzle
quebra-cabeças
(ke-brah-kah-BEY-sas)

train
trem
(TREM)

wagon
caminhão
(ca-mee-NYOWM)

puppet
fantoche
(fan-TOW-che)

skateboard
skate
(is-KEY-ite)

jump rope
pular corda
(poo-LAHR KOWR-dah)

ball
bola
(BOW-lah)

bat
bastão
(bas-TAUM)

window
janela
(jah-NAI-lah)

picture
fotografia
(fo-to-gra-FEE-uh)

lamp
lâmpada
(LAN-pah-dah)

dresser
cômoda
(KO-mo-dah)

curtain
cortina
(kor-TEE-nah)

blanket
cobertor
(ko-ber-TOR)

door
porta
(POWR-tah)

pillow
travesseiro
(trah-ve-SEY-ro)

bed
cama
(KA-ma)

rug
tapete
(tah-PEY-te)

13

bathtub
banheira
(ba-NYE-rah)

soap
sabonete
(sah-bo-NEY-te)

toilet
privada
(pree-VAH-dah)

toothbrush
escova de dentes
(es-CO-vah de DEYN-teys)

mirror
espelho
(es-PEY-lee-oh)

toothpaste
pasta de dentes
(PAHS-tah de DEYN-teys)

comb
pente
(PEYN-te)

sink
pia
(PEE-ah)

towel
toalha
(to-AH-lyah)

brush
escova
(es-CO-vah)

15

pot
panela
(pah-NAI-lah)

stove
fogão
(fo-GAUM)

bowl
tigela
(tee-JAI-lah)

oven
forno
(FOR-no)

16

refrigerator
refrigerador
(rey-free-jey-rah-DOR)

knife
faca
(FAH-cah)

table
mesa
(MEY-zah)

plate
prato
(PRAH-to)

spoon
colher
(co-LAIR)

fork
garfo
(GAHR-fo)

17

milk
leite
(LEY-te)

carrot
cenoura
(sey-NOU-rah)

bread
pão
(PAUM)

apple
maçã
(mah-SAN)

butter
manteiga
(man-TEY-gah)

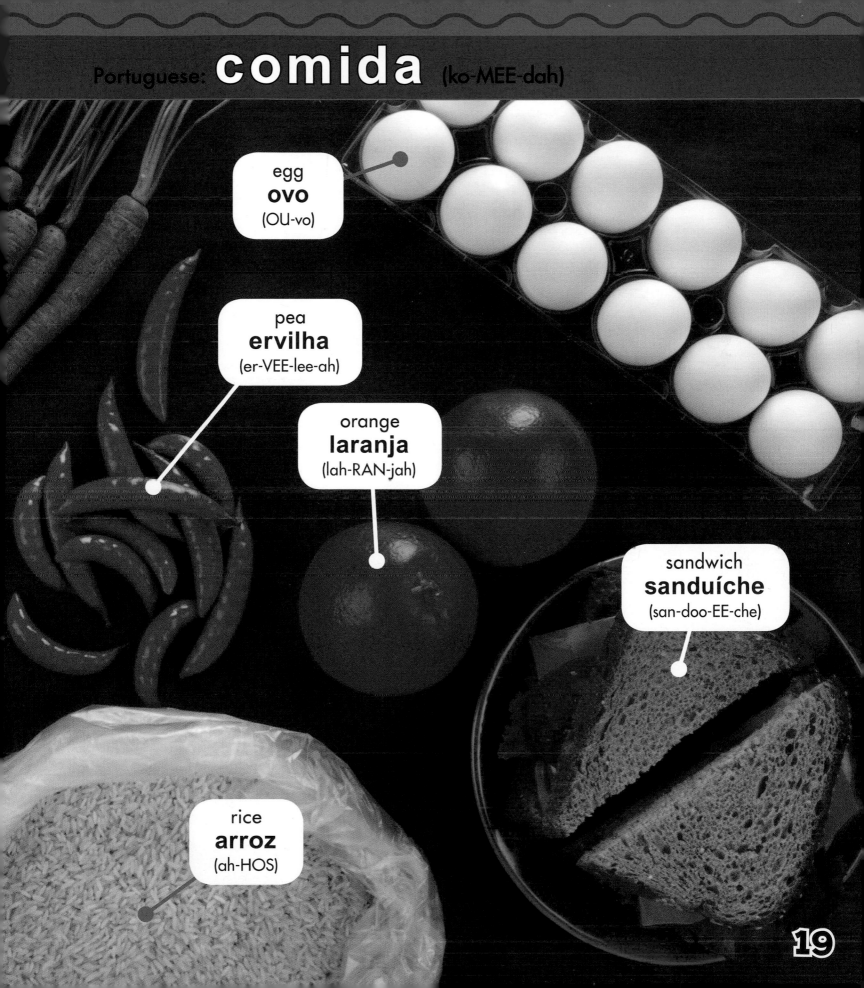

egg
ovo
(OU-vo)

pea
ervilha
(er-VEE-lee-ah)

orange
laranja
(lah-RAN-jah)

sandwich
sanduíche
(san-doo-EE-che)

rice
arroz
(ah-HOS)

tractor
trator
(trah-TOR)

hay
feno
(FEY-no)

fence
cerca
(CEYR-kah)

farmer
fazendeiro
(fah-zen-DEY-ro)

sheep
ovelha
(o-VEY-lyah)

pig
porco
(POR-ko)

horse
cavalo
(kah-VA-lo)

barn
celeiro
(se-LEY-ro)

cow
vaca
(VAH-kah)

chicken
galinha
(gah-LEE-nya)

leaf
folha
(FO-lee-ah)

butterfly
borboleta
(bor-bo-LEY-tah)

flower
flor
(FLOR)

shovel
pá
(PAH)

bird
pássaro
(PAH-sah-ro)

worm
verme
(VEHR-me)

22

plant
planta
(PLAN-tah)

grass
grama
(GRA-ma)

Edamame Green Soybean

Tohya

Glycine max

$2.99
Net Weight
15 grams

80 days
Warm season
crop - plant after
last chance of
spring frost

So high in
protein, it is
called "the meat
without bones".
Boiled, beans
are popped out
of the pod into
your mouth for
a culinary
delight!

dirt
lama
(LA-mah)

seed
semente
(sey-MEYN-te)

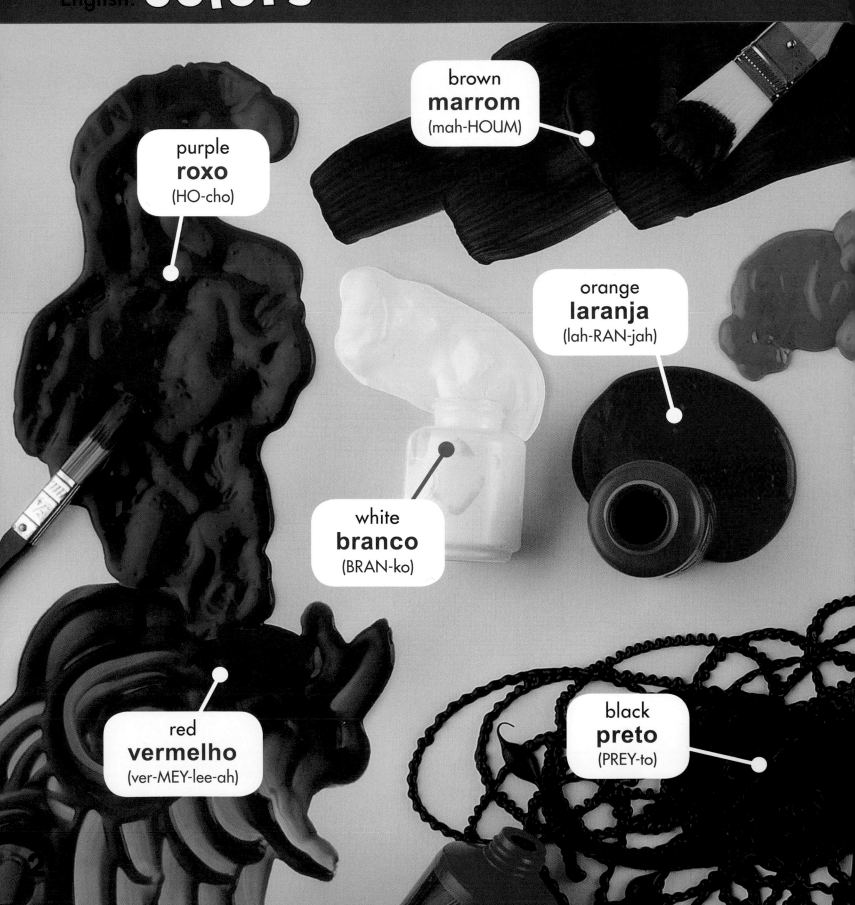

purple
roxo
(HO-cho)

brown
marrom
(mah-HOUM)

orange
laranja
(lah-RAN-jah)

white
branco
(BRAN-ko)

red
vermelho
(ver-MEY-lee-ah)

black
preto
(PREY-to)

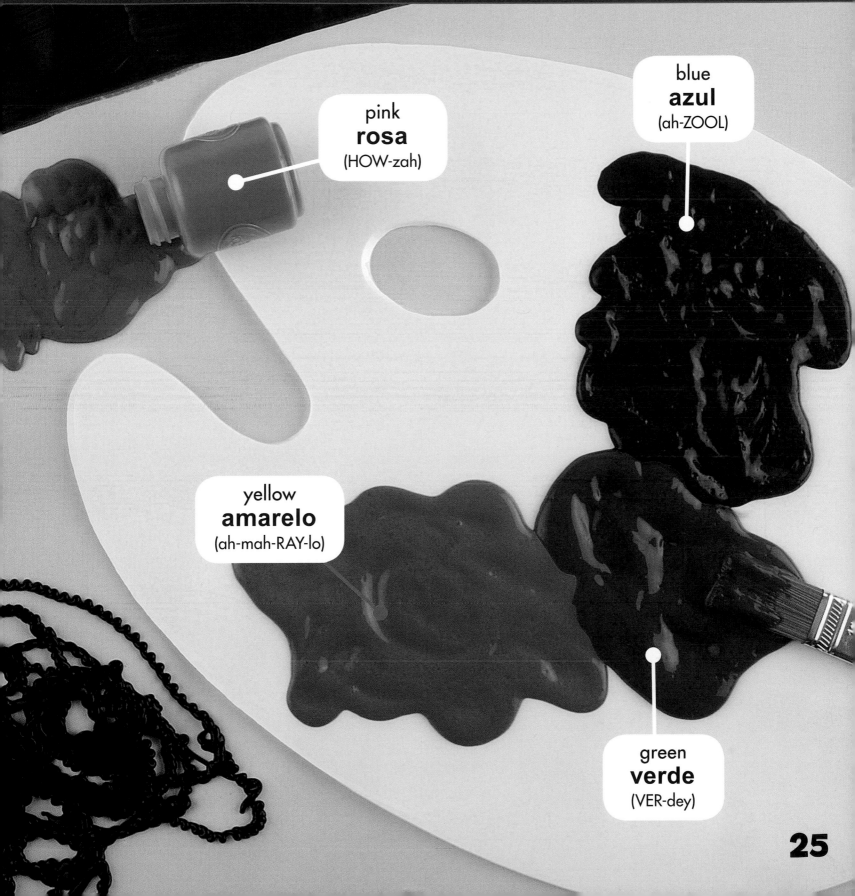

pink
rosa
(HOW-zah)

blue
azul
(ah-ZOOL)

yellow
amarelo
(ah-mah-RAY-lo)

green
verde
(VER-dey)

teacher
professor
(pro-fe-SOR)

book
livro
(LEE-vro)

pencil
lápis
(LAH-pees)

desk
mesa
(MEY-zah)

crayon
giz de cera
(GEES dey SEY-rah)

26

Portuguese: **sala de aula** (SA-lah dey AU-lah)

map
mapa
(MAH-pah)

clock
relógio
(he-LOH-gee-oh)

computer
computador
(kom-poo-tah-DOR)

chair
cadeira
(kah-DEY-rah)

paper
papel
(pah-PAI-oo)

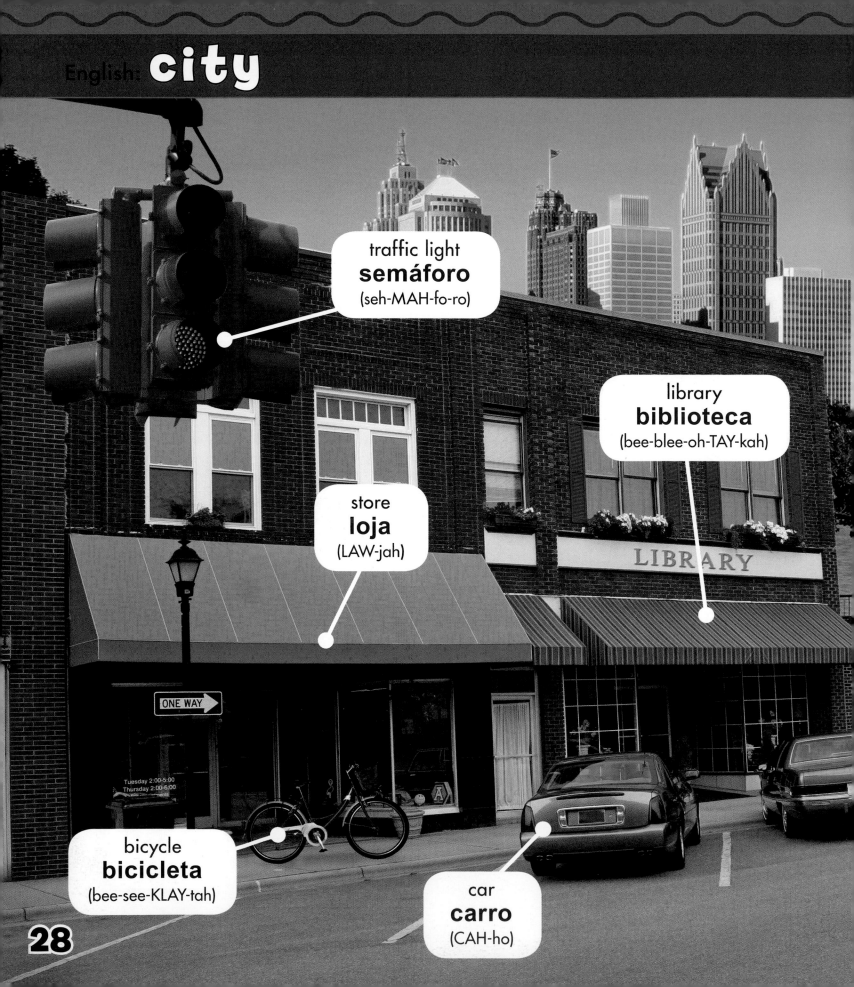

traffic light
semáforo
(seh-MAH-fo-ro)

library
biblioteca
(bee-blee-oh-TAY-kah)

store
loja
(LAW-jah)

LIBRARY

ONE WAY

Tuesday 2:00-5:00
Thursday 2:00-6:00

bicycle
bicicleta
(bee-see-KLAY-tah)

car
carro
(CAH-ho)

Numbers • **Números** (NOO-mey-rohs)

1. one • **um** (OOM)
2. two • **dois** (DO-is)
3. three • **três** (TREYS)
4. four • **quatro** (KUAH-tro)
5. five • **cinco** (CEEN-ko)

6. six • **seis** (SEYS)
7. seven • **sete** (SAI-te)
8. eight • **oito** (OI-to)
9. nine • **nove** (NOW-ve)
10. ten • **dez** (DAIS)

Useful Phrases • **Frases úteis** (FRA-zes OO-teys)

yes • **sim** (SEEM)

no • **não** (NAUM)

hello • **olá** (oh-LAH)

good-bye • **adeus** (a-DEY-us)

good morning • **bom dia** (BOM DEE-ah)

good night • **boa noite** (BO-ah NOY-te)

please • **por favor** (POR fah-VOR)

thank you • **obrigado/obrigada** (oh-bree-GAH-doh/oh-bree-GAH-dah)

excuse me • **desculpe-me** (des-COOL-pe-me)

My name is _____. • **Meu nome é** _____. (MEH-oo NOW-meh AY)

30

Read More

Amery, Heather. *First Thousand Words in Portuguese.*
London: Usborne Books, 2008.

Turhan, Sedat. *Milet Picture Dictionary: English-Portuguese.*
London: Milet Publishing, 2005.

Internet Sites

FactHound offers a safe, fun way to find Internet sites related to this book. All of the sites on FactHound have been researched by our staff.

Here's all you do:

Visit *www.facthound.com*

Type in this code: 9781429659659

Super-cool stuff! Check out projects, games and lots more at www.capstonekids.com

A+ Books are published by Capstone Press,
151 Good Counsel Drive, P.O. Box 669, Mankato, Minnesota 56002.
www.capstonepub.com

 Books published by Capstone Press are manufactured with paper
containing at least 10 percent post-consumer waste.

Library of Congress Cataloging-in-Publication Data
Kudela, Katy R.
    My first book of Portuguese words / by Katy R. Kudela.
    p. cm. — (A+ Books, Bilingual picture dictionaries)
    Includes bibliographical references.
     Summary: "Simple text paired with themed photos invite the reader to learn to speak Portuguese"—
Provided by publisher.
    ISBN 978-1-4296-5965-9 (library binding)
    ISBN 978-1-4296-6169-0 (paperback)
    1. Picture dictionaries, Portuguese. 2. Picture dictionaries, English. 3. Portuguese language—
Dictionaries, Juvenile—English. 4. English language—Dictionaries, Juvenile—Portuguese. I. Title. II. Series.
PC5333.K83 2011
469.3'21—dc22   2010029474

Credits
Lori Bye, designer; Wanda Winch, media researcher; Eric Manske, production specialist

Photo Credits
Capstone Studio/Gary Sundermeyer, cover (pig), 20 (farmer with tractor, pig)
Capstone Studio/Karon Dubke, cover (ball, sock), 1, 3, 4–5, 6–7, 8–9, 10–11, 12–13, 14–15,
    16–17, 18–19, 22–23, 24–25, 26–27
Image Farm, back cover, 1, 2, 31, 32 (design elements)
iStockphoto/Andrew Gentry, 28 (main street)
Photodisc, cover (flower)
Shutterstock/Adrian Matthiassen, cover (butterfly); David Hughes, 20 (hay); Eric Isselee,
    20–21 (horse); hamurishi, 28 (bike); Ievgeniia Tikhonova, 21 (chickens); Jim Mills, 29
    (stop sign); Kelli Westfal, 28 (traffic light); Margo Harrison, 20 (sheep); MaxPhoto, 21
    (cow and calf); Melinda Fawver, 29 (bus); Robert Elias, 20–21 (barn, fence); Vladimir
    Mucibabic, 28–29 (city skyline)

Note to Parents, Teachers, and Librarians
Learning to speak a second language at a young age has been shown to improve overall
academic performance, boost problem-solving ability, and foster an appreciation for other
cultures. Early exposure to language skills provides a strong foundation for other subject
areas, including math and reasoning. Introducing children to a second language can help
to lay the groundwork for future academic success and cultural awareness.

Printed in the United States of America in North Mankato, Minnesota.
092010   005933CGS11